The Obersalzberg and the Third Reich

Dear visitor!

This brochure will give you a survey of the drastic changes on the Obersalzberg. It has been tried to show how a formerly beautiful landscape was disfigured by houses and roads. Today only some remnants and ruins are to be seen. You will get an interesting glimpse of the past of the mountain. In 1877 Mauritia Mayer, the owner of the mountain health resort "Moritz", began to establish a modest guest-house, Berchtesgaden. At first he found shelter with his friend Dietrich Eckart, who was to become co-founder of the Nazi party NSDAP, in the Sonnenhaeusl on the Lockstein. Later he lived in a log cabin on the Obersalzberg where he finished his book "Mein Kampf" (= my struggle). He found friends and supporters among the locals and thus in 1928 could rent Haus Wachenfels. Five months after his seizure of power in 1933

which later was to become the "Platterhof". After World War I the Americans used the building as a hotel: The "Recreation Hotel General Walker".

In the times of Mauritia Mayer many illustrious people spent their summer vacations on the Obersalzberg.

Shortly after Hitler´s unsuccessful coup in Munich and after his release from Landsberg prison, the Fuehrer retired to Hitler bought the house and started to reconstruct it. His party friends followed him to the Obersalzberg and built their homes around Hitler´s Berghof. The laws settling the leaving of farms were ignored, the destruction of the idyll took its course. Under the control of Rudolf Hess the buildings and plots were "bought", old farmsteads were demolished and their owners were forced to settle somewhere else.

The picture on the previous page shows the former Bodner field with the Bodner farm on the left. The arrow points to the Tuerken Hotel, with the Marienhaeusl on the right and the Untersberg Mountain (1894 m) in the background. The precipices on the right are on Austrian territory. The hill in the middle distance is the Kneifel-spitze (1189 m). The Bodner field later became the site of the SS barracks with parade ground and underground shooting range.

OBERSALZBERG

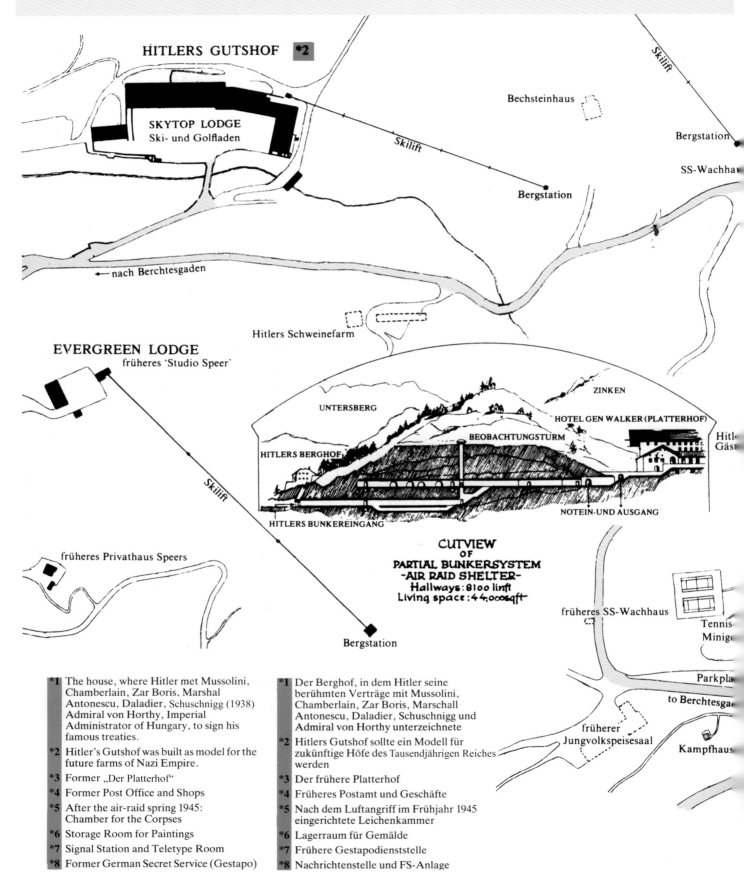

HITLERS GUTSHOF *2

SKYTOP LODGE
Ski- und Golfladen

Bechsteinhaus

Skilift

Bergstation

SS-Wachha

Skilift

Bergstation

← nach Berchtesgaden

Hitlers Schweinefarm

EVERGREEN LODGE
früheres 'Studio Speer'

ZINKEN

UNTERSBERG

HOTEL GEN WALKER (PLATTERHOF)

BEOBACHTUNGSTURM

HITLERS BERGHOF

Hitl
Gäst

Skilift

HITLERS BUNKEREINGANG

NOTEIN-UND AUSGANG

CUTVIEW
OF
PARTIAL BUNKERSYSTEM
-AIR RAID SHELTER-
Hallways: 8100 linft
Living space: 44.000 sqft

früheres Privathaus Speers

früheres SS-Wachhaus

Tennis-
Minige

Bergstation

Parkpla

to Berchtesga

früherer
Jungvolkspeisesaal

Kampfhaus

*1 The house, where Hitler met Mussolini, Chamberlain, Zar Boris, Marshal Antonescu, Daladier, Schuschnigg (1938) Admiral von Horthy, Imperial Administrator of Hungary, to sign his famous treaties.	*1 Der Berghof, in dem Hitler seine berühmten Verträge mit Mussolini, Chamberlain, Zar Boris, Marschall Antonescu, Daladier, Schuschnigg und Admiral von Horthy unterzeichnete
*2 Hitler's Gutshof was built as model for the future farms of Nazi Empire.	*2 Hitlers Gutshof sollte ein Modell für zukünftige Höfe des Tausendjährigen Reiches werden
*3 Former „Der Platterhof"	*3 Der frühere Platterhof
*4 Former Post Office and Shops	*4 Früheres Postamt und Geschäfte
*5 After the air-raid spring 1945: Chamber for the Corpses	*5 Nach dem Luftangriff im Frühjahr 1945 eingerichtete Leichenkammer
*6 Storage Room for Paintings	*6 Lagerraum für Gemälde
*7 Signal Station and Teletype Room	*7 Frühere Gestapodienststelle
*8 Former German Secret Service (Gestapo)	*8 Nachrichtenstelle und FS-Anlage

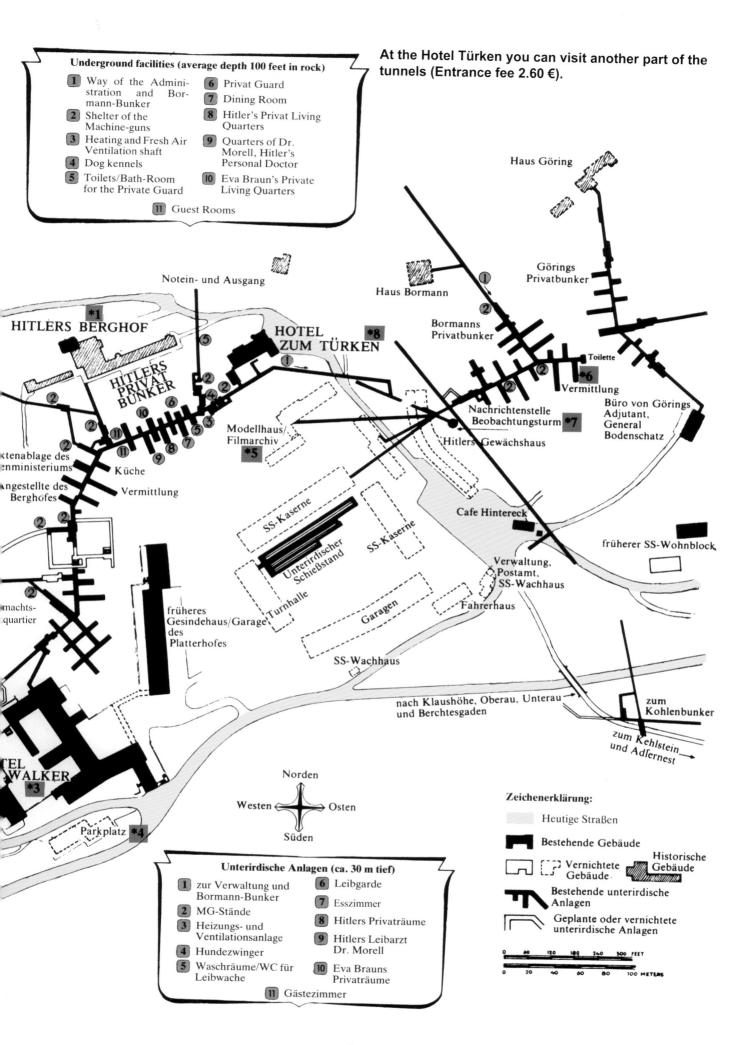

Underground facilities (average depth 100 feet in rock)

1. Way of the Administration and Bormann-Bunker
2. Shelter of the Machine-guns
3. Heating and Fresh Air Ventilation shaft
4. Dog kennels
5. Toilets/Bath-Room for the Private Guard
6. Privat Guard
7. Dining Room
8. Hitler's Privat Living Quarters
9. Quarters of Dr. Morell, Hitler's Personal Doctor
10. Eva Braun's Private Living Quarters
11. Guest Rooms

At the Hotel Türken you can visit another part of the tunnels (Entrance fee 2.60 €).

Haus Göring

Görings Privatbunker

Haus Bormann

Bormanns Privatbunker

Toilette

*6

Vermittlung

Büro von Görings Adjutant, General Bodenschatz

Nachrichtenstelle Beobachtungsturm *7

Hitlers Gewächshaus

Notein- und Ausgang

HITLERS BERGHOF

HITLERS PRIVAT BUNKER

HOTEL ZUM TÜRKEN

*8

*1

Modellhaus/ Filmarchiv *5

Cafe Hintereck

früherer SS-Wohnblock

...ktenablage des ...enministeriums

...angestellte des Berghofes

Küche

Vermittlung

SS-Kaserne

SS-Kaserne

Unterirdischer Schießstand

Verwaltung, Postamt, SS-Wachhaus

...machts- ...quartier

früheres Gesindehaus/Garage des Platterhofes

Turnhalle

Garagen

Fahrerhaus

SS-Wachhaus

nach Klaushöhe, Oberau, Unterau und Berchtesgaden

zum Kohlenbunker

...TEL ...WALKER

*3

Parkplatz *4

Norden

Westen ⟷ Osten

Süden

zum Kehlstein und Adlernest

Zeichenerklärung:

Heutige Straßen

Bestehende Gebäude

Vernichtete Gebäude

Historische Gebäude

Bestehende unterirdische Anlagen

Geplante oder vernichtete unterirdische Anlagen

0 60 120 180 240 300 FEET
0 20 40 60 80 100 METERS

Unterirdische Anlagen (ca. 30 m tief)

1. zur Verwaltung und Bormann-Bunker
2. MG-Stände
3. Heizungs- und Ventilationsanlage
4. Hundezwinger
5. Waschräume/WC für Leibwache
6. Leibgarde
7. Esszimmer
8. Hitlers Privaträume
9. Hitlers Leibarzt Dr. Morell
10. Eva Brauns Privaträume
11. Gästezimmer

3

Farms that had been owned by families for more than 300 years disappeared, just like villas and guest-houses. Hotel Klubheim, belonging to a Dresden club, the famous piano manufacturer´s house Villa Bechstein and other estates were confiscated and became part of the Nazi party assets. In 1936 Pension Moritz, three estates owned by the Association of Navy Officers, Hotel Antenberg, Upper and Lower Antenberg, Pension Lindenhoehe and 13 more villas and farms followed. End result of those purchases in 1937: 27 farms, private homes and guest-houses with a total of 428 hotel beds, and 650 acres of forests and fields. More than 400 people had to leave the mountain on short notice.

Bormann had a 27-meter-long fence erected around the "Fuehrer area" which expanded over 10 square kilometers. Only permit holders were authorized to enter it. Coming from Berchtesgaden, three guard houses had to be passed on the way to the Obersalzberg. Bormann´s later building mania was reaching its peak. Houses, roads and squares were constructed, rebuilt, completed or discarded again.

Some owners of farmsteads were paid generously, others were threatened with fines or with being sent to concentration camps so as to drive them away from the Obersalzberg.

Left: Clearing of a guest-house, about 200 m away from Hitler´s Berghof.
To the right, in the bend of the road below the restaurant, the remains of the "Lochner mill" can be seen.

Bottom: The Obersalzberg before Hitler. On the left the Bodner farm with its gently undulating fields. Below the farmhouse is the restaurant "Tuerken", behind it Haus Wachenfeld which was to become Hitler´s Berghof.
The arrow points to the site of the later SS barracks.

Hitler´s House

In former times, the term "Berghof" meant a well-organized and rather large mountain estate. Having been remodelled several times, Haus Wachenfels could no longer be called that.

With Hitler´s rise to power the Berghof began to be changed. The first minor alterations were carried out by the well-known architect Degano who managed to preserve the alpine style. As Hitler himself designed the blueprints, it was sometimes difficult for the architect to satisfy his customer. But at that time there were only minor alterations as yet. After Hitler had become Chancellor of the Reich, more and more Nazi friends visited the Obersalzberg. They stayed in nearby guest-houses. Initially, Rudolf Hess negotiated with the then estate owners, but then he was assigned political duties, and it was Martin Bormann´s turn. He was given overall control on the Obersalzberg as far as construction work was concerned. The first house he undertook to remodel was Hitler´s Berghof. Another storey was added, and the building was extensively enlarged. A flight of steps led up to the Gothic reception hall with its marble columns. From here one could get to the famous conference room which boasted a large window front that could be removed. Then there were the hall, the vestibule, a dining-room, a guards´ room, a room for the staff and a big kitchen. Two rooms were reserved for Hitler´s adjutants.

The second floor held Hitler´s living-rooms and bedrooms and some guest rooms. The garages were in the basement, and beneath those were the cellars containing the heating system as well as a bowling alley.

Only the most expensive material was used: windows framed in lead, furniture in Baroque and Biedermeier style, exquisite lamps, marble, precious wood, natural stones and tiled stoves. Valuable paintings and books, tapestries and expensive carpets completed the furnishing of the rooms.

Even before starting to remodel the house Bormann had the road leading from Berchtesgaden up to the Obersalzberg enlarged. In addition, a new road was built from Oberau.

Top:
Hitler´s Berghof, situated at 3000 feet above sea level at the foot of the Hoher Goell mountain, after being reconstructed for the third time.
The large window of the conference room which could be removed can be clearly seen.
To the right the big terrace.
Beneath it were the garages and the bowling alley.

5.

An interesting photograph:
Haus Wachenfeld in 1924.
The house was sold by Kommerzienrat Winter from Buxtehude to Hitler´s sister (3).
The Tuerken Hotel (1) on the left, the Bodner farm (2) a little higher up, the summit of the Hoher Goell (2522 m) towering above. To the right the Kehlstein mountain (1834 m), as yet without the Eagle´s Nest.

Daily thousands of visitors came to see Hitler. A fence prevented people from coming too near to the house. Hitler´s personal photographer Hoffmann and Propaganda Minister Goebbels presented the Obersalzberg as an idyll where the "people´s chancellor" Adolf Hitler was within reach.

Page 9, top left: A boat trip on Lake Koenigssee. The spires of St. Bartholomae´s in the background. Top right: Hitler posing as a man fond of children. Bottom: Hitler shaking hands with visitors who collected even the sand on which he had been standing to take home as a souvenir.

Aerial photo of Haus Wachenfeld before it was reconstructed for the last time.

Centre:
Nobody could get to the Berghof without a permit. On the left the last guard house in the restricted zone.
Its foundation walls can still be seen.

Bottom: The massive Berghof as it finally looked.

Page 11, top:
Hitler´s study in the Berghof. It was lavishly furnished.

Page 11, bottom:
The audience chamber.

10

Page 12, top: Whenever Hitler stayed on the Obersalzberg he went for long walks. The "people´s chancellor" liked appearing affable, as can be seen in this picture in which he is talking to the hunters of the surrounding communities.

Page 12, bottom: Adjutant Wilhem Brueckner opening the gate for Hitler. Behind them the youth leader of the Reich, Baldur von Schirach.

Conversations in front of the Dietrich Eckart House. To the left Hermann Goering, to the right Adolf Hitler, between them Field Marshal v. Blomberg.

Today the German Alpine Road, which originally was to run across the mountain plateau of the Steinernes Meer, ends behind the building. From here, the Christophorus High School and the Jenner cable-car can be reached in a few minutes.

14

Eva Braun

Eva Braun was a retiring, quiet lady´s companion at the Berghof. Her probably greatest desire - to become Mrs Adolf Hitler - was fulfilled under tragic circumstances in the chancellery of the Reich in Berlin, shortly before its destruction, on April 29, 1945. Goebbels and Bormann were witnesses at the marriage ceremony. One day later Adolf Hitler and Eva Braun committed suicide.

The propaganda picture shows Eva Braun and Hitler with the children of a friend. It was published world-wide with the capton "Adolf Hitler´s children".

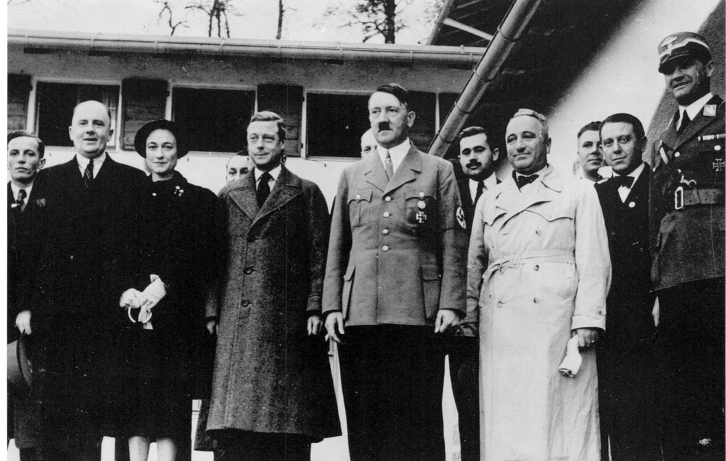

This time they were more thorough in their work of destruction. The heavy bombs (up to 5000 kg each) tore the Obersalzberg to pieces for a full hour. Hitler's Berghof was badly hit. The tin roof was hanging down, the extension building was completely destroyed. The houses of Bormann and Goering were covered by sulphur-like smoke. The SS barracks were totally destroyed, too.

The "people's hotel", the Platterhof, was hit, but not as badly as other houses. The Tuerken Hotel was completely bombed out.
Six people lost their lives. The huge bunker system survived the attack. The Eagle's Nest remained undamaged. All the building material was destroyed, innumerable vehicles and machines were ruined. Then there was silence.
When, hours later, the smoke cleared, the extent of the bombing became visible. On the same day there was an air-raid on the town of Bad Reichenhall. 200 people lost their lives there.

Top left: A reconnaissance picture taken from a British Lancaster bomber. The square (centre) are the SS barracks.
To the right are the drivers' quarters, in the front is the Platterhof. The arrow points to the Berghof.

Top right: Years after the air-raid: the same picture of destruction.

The big picture shows British Lancaster bombers of the 617th squadron above Lake Walchensee on their way to the Obersalzberg.

A picture of destruction:
The Berghof after being bombed out, behind it the Tuerken Hotel.
Bormann´s house (top, left) is bombed out, too. Remains of the green-
house can be seen above the Tuerken Hotel.
This picture was not taken immediately after the air-raid, as the writings
on the walls clearly show.

A view from "Goering´s Hill" of Bormann´s house and the ruins of the Berghof. To the left the building of the kindergarten, behind it the barracks.

Page 23, top and center: American GI´s in front of the window and on the flight of steps of the Berghof.

The ruin of the Berghof was left standing on the Obersalzberg as a warning until 1952 when it was demolished on the urging of the Bavarian government under Prime Minister Hoegner.

Top:
The Tuerken Hotel which was rebuilt under most difficult circumstances in 2003.

Bottom:
The access road to the Berghof. The building was blown up in 1952. The small path lower down leads to the big flight of steps where Hitler used to receive his guests. In connection with the construction of a new hotel on the Eckerbichl the area is being re-naturalized.

The last remnants of the Berghof:
The eastern wall is more or less an extension of the big flight of steps
leading up to the house.

View from the top of the flight of steps
towards the Untersberg mountain.
The green belongs to the present golf
course. In winter this is a skiing area.

View from the area of the Berghof
back to the Tuerken Hotel
and the access road.

Landhaus Goering

According to authentic statements Reichsmarschall Hermann Goering was not as domineering and arrogant as Bormann on the Obersalzberg. For some time, he had owned a small house above the Berghof. Hitler allowed him to rebuild and enlarge it. Goering was intelligent enough not to compete with Bormann. Thus the big country house was built on the hill named after Goering. It held some precious objects. The private swimming pool indicates that the house boasted every kind of luxury inside, too. As to its situation, it probably stood on the most beautiful spot of the Obersalzberg. Today the new luxury hotel stands in solitary splendour there. Goering liked bright, polished ceilings, mosaics with flowers and animals in natural colors. His wife Emmy was a successful actress. The family generally did not often meet the Bormanns, Hitler and Eva Braun socially.

Later the house was rebuilt twice, and finally it was a splendid building which nevertheless went well with the landscape. After the air-raid the main building was completely destroyed, whereas the last building to be added was only slightly damaged. The furnishings, windows and doors were looted. Until 2002, a small water hole reminded visitors of the swimming pool. Behind the house a path led about 20 m lower down to the entrance of Hermann Goering´s bunker system. This system of tunnels has no connection with that belonging to Hitler´s house.

As minister responsible for the forests of the Reich, Goering decidedly had a closeness to forests. He had a hunting lodge built in the Roeth, above Lake Obersee. Its foundation walls can still be seen. There he enjoyed hunting.

Goering´s house. It was built in Upper-Bavarian style and had a shingled roof weighed down with stones.

Right:
Hermann Goering was born in 1893. During World War I he was a successful fighter pilot. In 1922 he joined the Nazi party; in 1923 he was wounded while taking part in Hitler´s coup d'état. He was pretty fat, caused by a wound during the first world war. In 1933 he became prime minister of Prussia. He was in charge of the German Air Force, and in 1940 he became Reichsmarschall. In the Nuremberg trials he was sentenced to death, but committed suicide.

Hermann Goering and his wife Emmy on the terrace of his house, together with a lion cub.

27

Left:
Goering´s house with its outdoor swimming pool before it was reconstructed for the last time; in the valley the houses of Unterau and the road to Salzburg can be seen.

Bottom:
Nazi VIP´s enjoying themselves on the Obersalzberg.

Hermann Goering´s study.

Goering on horseback as a hunter, high above Lake Obersee in the area of the Teufelshörner (Devils' Horns). He had a number of ibex released there in order to get a population which could be hunted.
The animals were transported to the station at the bottom of the cable-car at Lake Obersee in wooden boxes and taken up to the Roeth.

Propaganda photos taken by Heinrich Hoffmann in order to gloss over life around Hitler and to lead the German people to believe in the "idyll" in the mountains.

Görings abgerissene Jagdhütte
Ein Wert von 42 000 RM zerstört

A report from 1949 about the destruction of Goering´s hunting lodge. The foundation walls and part of the cable-car at Lake Obersee are still there.

Warum scheut sie eine sachliche Diskussion, der unsere Zeitung jederzeit offensteht?

Als Sprachrohr der Oeffentlichkeit können wir nicht stillschweigend zusehen, wenn Volksvermögen willkürlich und ohne jede zwingende Notwendigkeit vernichtet wird. Noch dazu, wenn es — wie in diesem Falle — als bewirtschaftete Unterkunftshütte einen rentablen Ertrag bringen könnte.

Es gelang nach wochenlangen Bemühungen, ein Bild der abgerissenen Göring-Jagdhütte aufzutreiben. Sie verkörperte einen Friedenswert von 42 000 RM. Selbst der verschwenderische Göring, der anscheinend nur 20 000 RM verausgaben wollte, soll über die hohen Kosten ungehalten gewesen sein. Eine bei der Forstbehörde beschäftigte Person, die nicht genannt sein will, weil ihr sonst Entlassung droht, schrieb uns u. a.: „Ihr Artikel über die Göringhütte entspricht den Tatsachen und der wahren Volksmeinung. Weite Kreise sind empört... Mit Spitzhauen und Sapinen wurden die Lärchenholzvertäfelungen herausgerissen und an Ort und Stelle verbrannt... Mein soziales Gewissen zwingt mich, Ihnen zu schreiben. Erkundigen Sie sich am besten über die Gewerkschaft, bei den Forstarbeitern und Lehrlingen, die beim Abreißen beschäftigt waren, und Sie werden meine Angaben vollauf bestätigt finden!"

Wir fragen heute und fordern Aufklärung, die auf Grund des neuen Beamtengesetzes gar nicht mehr verweigert werden darf: Mit welchen Geldern wurden die Abbrucharbeiten bezahlt? Wer hat Geld zum Abreißen, während die dringendsten Mittel für den Aufbau fehlen?

Es soll im Zusammenhang mit dieser Angelegenheit eine bezeichnende Aeußerung gefallen sein, die — wenn auch im genauen Wortlaut nicht mehr einwandfrei überprüfbar — doch die Einstellung kennzeichnet: Bevor Alpenverein oder Naturfreunde in Regen, Landtal oder Röth eine Hütte bekämen, würde sie eher angezündet. Man denkt da unwillkürlich an ein trotzköpfiges kleines Kind, das nach Hause kommt und triumphierend ruft: „Aetsch, Mama, jetzt habe ich mir die Hände erfroren, weil du mir keine Handschuhe gabst!"

Das Verhalten der Forstbehörde veranlaßt uns, heute an einen Vorfall zu erinnern, den wir bei unserer letzten Veröffentlichung am 21. März bewußt verschwiegen, um nicht unerfreuliche Polemiken anzuzetteln. Es handelt sich um folgende Tatsachen:

In der Nacht vom 2. auf 3. Mai 1946 brannte unter mysteriösen Umständen die geräumige, ... Krieg vom Reichenhaller Gebirgsjäger-Regiment erbaute Blaueishütte ab. Der Hüttenwart der benachbarten Blaueishütte des Alpenvereins war wegen einer Bergung am Watzmann abwesend. Es herrschte schlechte Witterung. Keinerlei Touristenverkehr wurde an diesem Tage beobachtet. Es kam auch zu keinem Gewitter mit Blitzen, die eine Entzündung hätten herbeiführen können. Die Hütte brannte bis auf die Grundmauern ab. Nach Auffassung der Ramsauer Bevölkerung wurde die Untersuchung der Brandursache eigenartig schnell abgebrochen.

Das Zerstörungswerk des Feuers war nicht genug. An der Hütte war ziemlich viel gemauert, und man hätte die Küche und einige Räume wieder ausbauen können. Das mußte unbedingt vermieden werden. Das Forstamt ließ daher im Herbst 1947 die Mauern so gründlich sprengen, daß die Hütte nun restlos vernichtet ist. Im Schweiße vieler Arbeitsstunden war sie in fast 2000 Meter Höhe mühsam erbaut und hätte auf Jahrzehnte hinaus als touristischer Stützpunkt dienen können.

Dies sind nur die nachweisbaren Tatsachen. Sollte sie jemand bezweifeln, so können wir noch mit einigen zusätzlichen Enthüllungen aufwarten.

Die Forstbehörde schweigt. Wir schweigen nicht. In unserer Ausgabe vom 21. März brachten wir unter dem Titel „Wer ließ Görings Jagdhütte abreißen? Ein unvergessener Willkürakt" einen Artikel, der in unserem gesamten Verbreitungsgebiet großes Aufsehen erregte. Es wurde überall begrüßt, daß wir diese Angelegenheit ebenso sachlich wie schonungslos aufgriffen. Wir bekamen zustimmende Zuschriften und unter „Leserbriefe" erinnerte W. Lossen an ein leider schon fast vergessenes ähnliches Vandalenwerk der Forstbehörde, durch das vor 30 Jahren das Priesberg-Jagdhaus des Prinzregenten Luitpold vernichtet wurde, damit es ja nicht eine alpine Vereinigung als touristischen Stützpunkt bekommen könnte.

Wir haben lange auf eine Entgegnung gewartet. Sie kam nicht. Das Schweigen der Forstbehörde zeugt von schlechtem Gewissen.

After the air-raid of 25 April, 1945. The photos were taken several years after the raid. Looters even removed the tiles in the bathroom of Goering´s house. At that time, understandably, everything was of use.

Page 33, bottom right: View from the house via the swimming-pool toward the SS barracks.

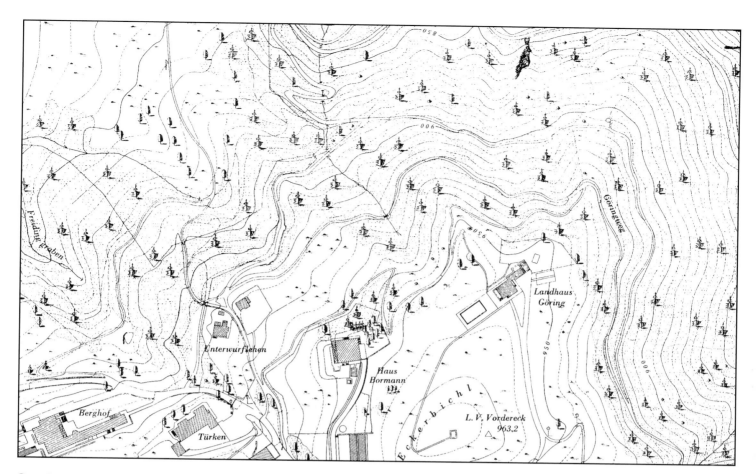

South view of Goering´s house after being completely bombed out. During the last months of the war Goering had the ground floor filled with concrete. Beneath it was the air-raid shelter: The bombs could not destroy the concrete block. It also survived demolition and was only removed in 2002. After invasion, the Americans raised the Stars and Stripes on the brow of "Goering´s Hill" (formerly Eckerbichl) above the house. Today this is the site of the new luxury hotel.

Pos. Goering house

Der "alte Obersalzberg" vor 19...
THE OLD OBERSALZBERG BEVOR 1933
LE ANCIEN OBERSALZBERG AVANT 1933

Bormann´s house was covered with wooden boards so that it looked like a country house. Inside it was luxuriously furnished. It stood to the left and above the Tuerken Hotel. Today the site can only be guessed. Dense bushes have grown there. There is nothing left of the house.

Bottom, right: A historical postcard: "Weihnachtsschützen (Christmas riflemen) in front of the Berghof".

Page 39: Building material was scarce; procuring material at Haus Bormann.

Pages 36/37: Postcard of the Obersalzberg.

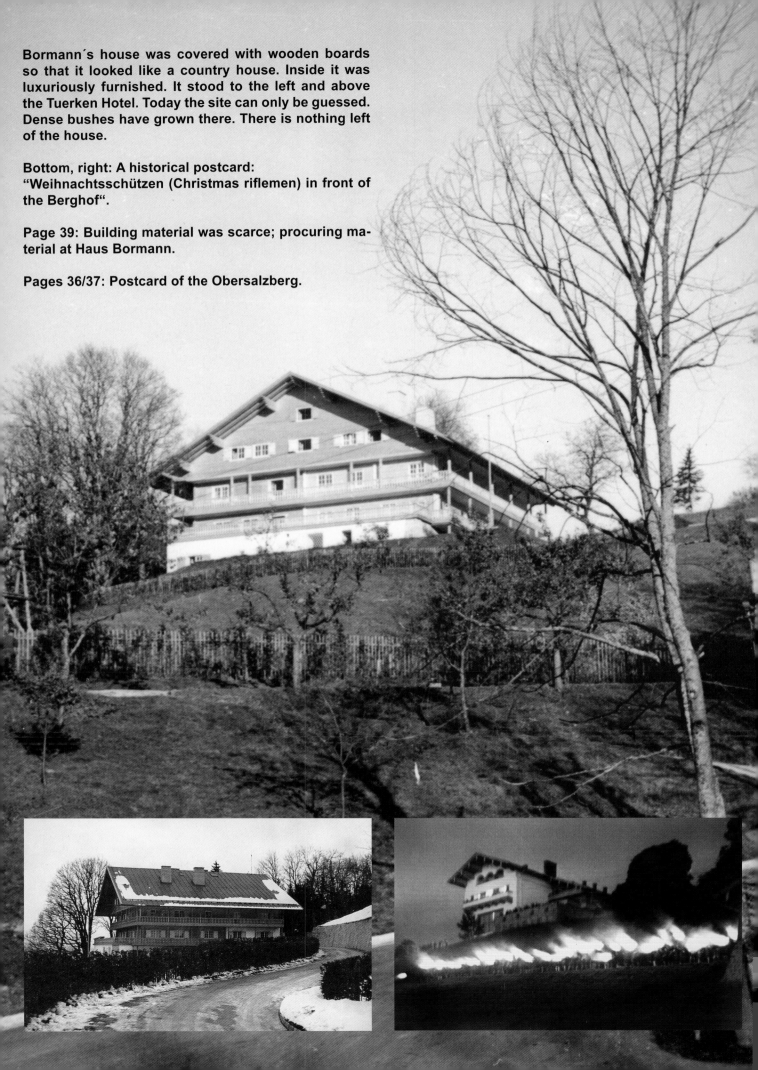

Martin Bormann

Bormann followed Hitler to the Obersalzberg and obtained an immense influence over the Fuehrer. By and by he seized control over all construction work. Towards the end of the war he continued building, finally at Klaushoehe and Buchenhoehe. Procuring material was no problem for him as everything happened under Hitler´s direct order. Due to his inexhaustible energy and his well-functioning offices he was always perfectly informed about everything. He would have liked to fulfil Hitler´s wishes before they were uttered. The members of site supervision were afraid of him as he easily lost his temper, and they always really had problems with him. His habit to make all his decisions at night did not make things easy for his followers.

On his orders the former sanatorium of Dr Seitz was rebuilt as a country house for himself from which he looked as a „guardian" over all the other houses. It cannot be denied that Bormann had taste. According to reports, the children´s rooms, for example, were more beautiful than the rooms of fairy princes. He knew perfectly well how to make use of the authority Hitler accorded to him, and also how to make use of Hitler´s orders. The furnishing of the Gutshof is worth mentioning here. Having been a farmer before, it was a temptation to Bormann to show off as a lord of the manor now.

He did not have to account for its profitability. Bormann was busy breeding Haflinger horses, a species that is still used by the mountain troops in Bad Reichenhall. About 80 mares were to bring in most of the profit. In order to prove himself in the eyes of his model Adolf Hitler, he also kept 80 milking cows and 100 pigs in newly constructed buildings. 200 acres of meadows and farmland also belonged to the Gutshof. Due to the rough climate and the altitude the soil yielded only little grain. From a financial point of view the Guthof was a failure. It was only the must and apple press that brought in a little profit at all. The apples that were pressed at the Gutshof were bought on Bormann´s orders in all parts of the Reich. In spite of the mean profit, he had the Gutshof enlarged again and again so that later it resembled more a manor house than a farmstead.

During the air-raid the Gutshof was only slightly damaged. Until about 1994 the Americans used it as an "Armed Forces Recreation Area" (AFRC). Today, ski lifts and golf course, which are open to the public, are very popular.

Top: View of the Gutshof from the balcony of the Berghof. At the bottom of the picture can be seen the last guard house before the inner sector of the restricted area. Berchtesgaden in the valley, the Lattengebirge in the background.
Bottom: The site of the later Gutshof is wonderful. Many farmers had to leave their farms in order to make room for the Nazi rulers. The farmhouse on the right was used as a pig sty by Bormann. The arrow marks the Teahouse on the Mooslahnerkopf, where Hitler and his entourage went for walks almost daily, from there to be driven back to the Berghof.

List of buildings at Obersalzberg with a description of conditions following the Air Raid of April 25th, 1945

Obersalzberg / Berchtesgaden

Before 1933 (Name of last owner)	1933 - 1945		After 1945	After 2002
1. Scheberlehen (Walch Johann)	demolished		US Armed Forces golf course and ski area	Golf course (since 1955) and skiing area (since 1990) also for non-Americans. Owner: Free State of Bavaria leaseholder: Gewerbegrund Projektentwicklungsgesellschaft
2. Fichtenhäusl (Rasp Franz)	demolished			
3. Mooslehen (Rasp Franz)	demolished			
4. Beim Breiler (Angerer Thomas)	demolished			
5. In der Brandstatt (Irlinger Josef - Hölzl Anton)	demolished			
5a. Obertallehen (Irlinger Jakob)	demolished			
6. Sonnen-Köpfl (Cornelius Maria)	demolished			
7. Weissenlehen (Kastner Elise - Bechstein Edwin)	demolished 12. Gutshof		rebuilt as U.S. Armed Forces recreational hotel	
8. Villa Bechstein (Bechstein Edwin)	1. remodeled as accommodations for VIP guests (Party leaders, Goebbels, Mussolini)		1945 destroyed	
9. Freiding (Rasp Michael - Emilie v. Leignitz)	demolished			
10. Unterwurf (Geheimrat Schmidtlein Maria)	remodeled for administration		1945 destroyed	
11. Mitterwurf (Schwarz Bruno)	demolished			
12. Oberwurf (Hölzl Josef)	demolished			
13. Vordereck, Forsthaus	demolished			
14. Priv. house (Dr. Seitz Richard)	2. Bormann house		1945 destroyed	
Eckerbichl (Grund vom Vordereck, Forstamt)	3. Görings' house with swimming pool		1945 destroyed	Mountain Resort Hotel Obersalzberg
15. Childrens' Sanatorium with chapel (Dr. Seitz Richard)	demolished	4. green house	1945 destroyed	
16. Stables (Dr. Seitz Richard)	demolished			
17. Gasthof Hintereck (Kurz Peter)	demolished			demolished
18. Hinterecklehen (Hölzl Johann)	demolished	5. Adjutants building 6. Personnel Quarters	remains standing	
19. Fire Department	demolished		bus terminal	
20. Eckerbrunn (Walch Josef)	demolished			
21. Georgihäusl (Walch Georg)	demolished			
22. Haus Hudler (Hudler Anna)	demolished			
23. Haus Hess (Dr. Hess Johannes)	demolished			
24. Marienhäusl (Gräfin v. Rüxleben Cornelia)	demolished 9. administration building (Kindergarten and modelhouse)		1945 demolished	
25. Bodnerfeld Skigelände mit Sprungschanze	7. SS-baracks built 1941, Bodnerfeld		1945 demolished, soccer field	bunker system and foundations uncovered and filled; renaturalized
26. Bodnerlehen (Brandner Balthasar / Hudler Anna)	demolished			
27. Hotel Türken - früher Jakobsbichl (Schuster Karl)	8. remodeled as command HQ of RSD/ State Security Service		1945 badly damaged, rebuilt by original owner	
28. Haus Wachenfeld ruins (Winter Margarethe from Buxtehude) 1916 built, 1933 sold to Hitler	10. 1933 - 1934 remodeled Later rebuilt as "Berghof"		1945 destroyed, 1952 blown up	remains of completely removed

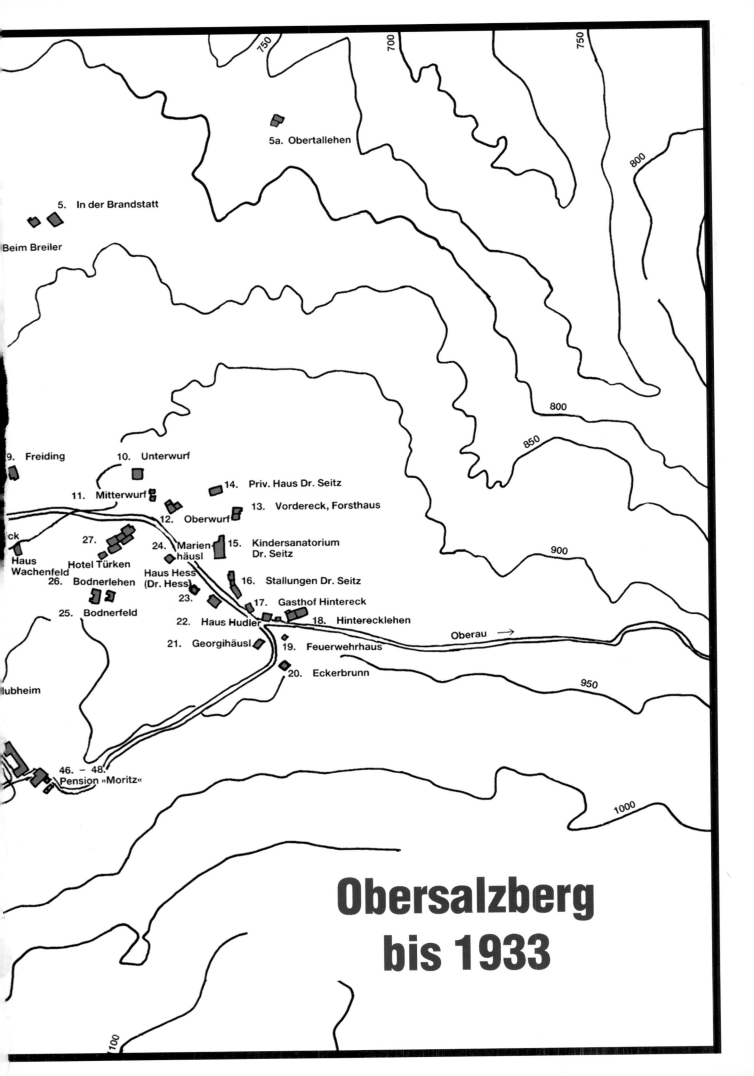

5a. Obertallehen

5. In der Brandstatt

Beim Breiler

9. Freiding

10. Unterwurf

11. Mitterwurf

14. Priv. Haus Dr. Seitz

13. Vordereck, Forsthaus

12. Oberwurf

27.

ck

Haus
Wachenfeld

Hotel Türken

24. Marien-
häusl

15. Kindersanatorium
Dr. Seitz

26. Bodnerlehen

Haus Hess
(Dr. Hess)

16. Stallungen Dr. Seitz

23.

17. Gasthof Hintereck

25. Bodnerfeld

22. Haus Hudler

18. Hinterecklehen

21. Georgihäusl

19. Feuerwehrhaus

Oberau →

lubheim

20. Eckerbrunn

46. – 48.
Pension »Moritz«

**Obersalzberg
bis 1933**

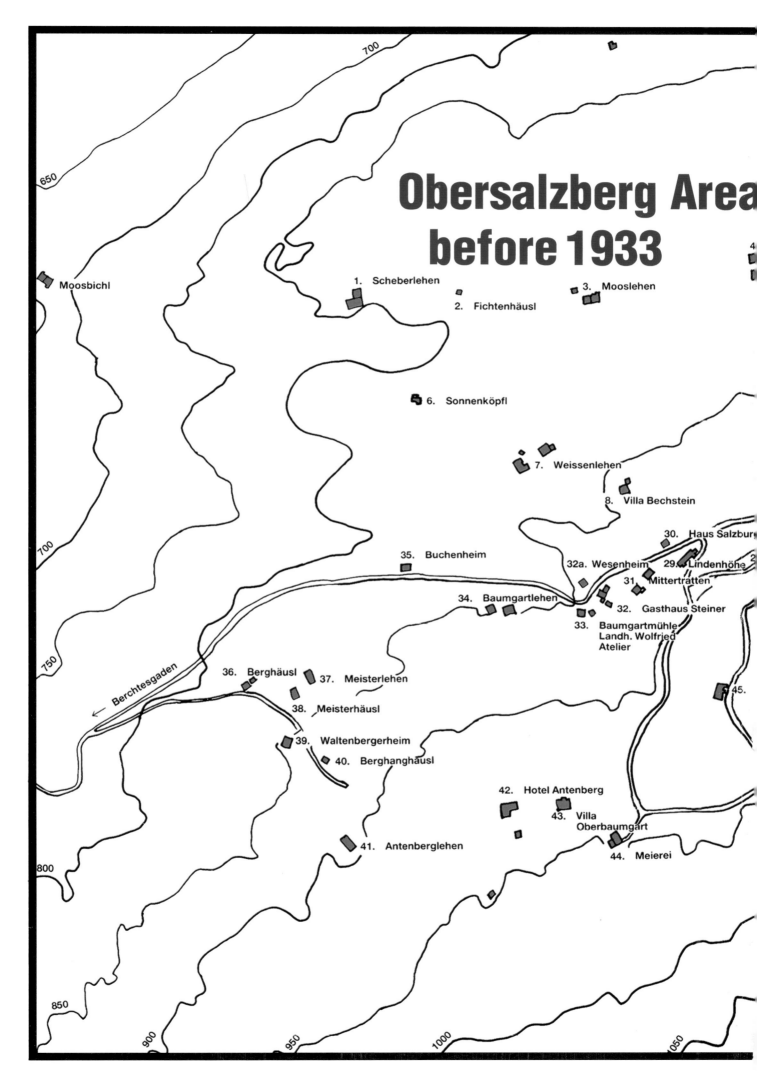

Obersalzberg Area
before 1933

Moosbichl

1. Scheberlehen
2. Fichtenhäusl
3. Mooslehen

6. Sonnenköpfl

7. Weissenlehen

8. Villa Bechstein

30. Haus Salzburg

35. Buchenheim

32a. Wesenheim   29. Lindenhöhe
31. Mittertratten

34. Baumgartlehen

32. Gasthaus Steiner

33. Baumgartmühle
Landh. Wolfried
Atelier

45.

36. Berghäusl   37. Meisterlehen

38. Meisterhäusl

39. Waltenbergerheim

40. Berghanghäusl

42. Hotel Antenberg

43. Villa
Oberbaumgart

41. Antenberglehen

44. Meierei

Berchtesgaden

700

650

700

750

800

850

900

950

1000

1050

Before 1933 (Name of last owner)		1933 – 1945		After 1945	After 2002
29.	Lindenhöhe (Geschwister Kaufmann)	demolished			
30.	Haus Salzburgblick (Zotz Martin)	demolished			
31.	Mittertratten, Schreinerei (Rappold)	demolished			
32.	Gasthaus Steiner (Kurz Johann)	demolished			
32a.	Wesenheim (Witting-Holstein)	demolished			
33.	Baumgartmühle (Lochner Wolfgang) Landh. Wolfried (Lochner Wolfgang jun.) Atelier (Lochner Michael)	demolished			
34.	Baumgartlechen (Carl v. Linde)	demolished 11. Gutshof farm		ruin	
35.	Buchenheim (Paulsen Claudius)	demolished			
36.	Berghäusel (Lochner Michael)	demolished			
37.	Meisterlehen (Walch Anton – Koller Anton)	demolished			
38.	Meisterhäusl (Koller Anton)	demolished			
39.	Waltenbergerheim (Sandner Norbert)	13. taken over by Reich Minister Speer (Speers' studio built below)		remains standing	
40.	Berghanghäusl (Fendt Ludwig)	remains standing			
41.	Antenberglehen	owner: Navy officers' club	demolished	14. workers barracks	1945 destroyed	
42.	Hotel Antenberg Naval rehabilitation center		demolished			
43.	Villa Oberbaumgart		demolished	15. movie theater	ruin of movie theater (wood components taken to munich and rebuilt as emergency church)	
44.	Meierei (vom) Hotel Antenberg)		16. rebuilt as a Youth rehab. center used for war home industry 17. built as "Kampfhäusl"		1945 destroyed	Information center Obersalzberg
45.	Clubheim (Arnoldscher Pensionsverein Dresden)	18. 1935 Party guest house		damaged by bombing (ruin)	
46. - 48.	Pension "Moritz" Formerly "Steinhaus" farm owned by Johann Hofreiter. Acquired by Moritz Mayer in 1877 and continued as a farm and a small hotel (known from 1878 on as "Pension Moritz"). Remodeled and partially rebuilt several times in the years that followed. After M. Mayer's death in 1897 her sister Antonie Mayer took over till 1921. From this time on owned by Dr. Joseph, then by Paul Dressel. Last owner: Bruno Buchner till sale in 1936.	19. 1936 rebuilt as Platterhof 1938 demolished and rebuilt as "Volkshotel" annex mountain inn 1943 veteran's hospital and home		1945 destroyed rebuilt as US Armed Forces recreational hotel	demolished with the exception of „Skyline Room"
		20. personnel building (barracks on Platterhof hill)		1945 destroyed 1981 dismantled	Buses to the Eagle´s Nest
		21. store and post office		1945 destroyed	
49. Klauslehen, Hammerlehen, Earlerhäusl (not shown on this map)		demolished 22. accomodations for Gov't employees and workers		1945 destroyed (partly standing)	
50. Buchenlehen, Wagnerlehen, Fürstenbichl (not shown on this map)		demolished 23. accomodations for Gov't employees and workers plus extra supplies facilities		1945 destroyed (partly standing) 1985 asthma cener built	
		24. coal bunker		1945 destroyed (ruin)	
		25. coal bunker		1945 destroyed (ruin)	

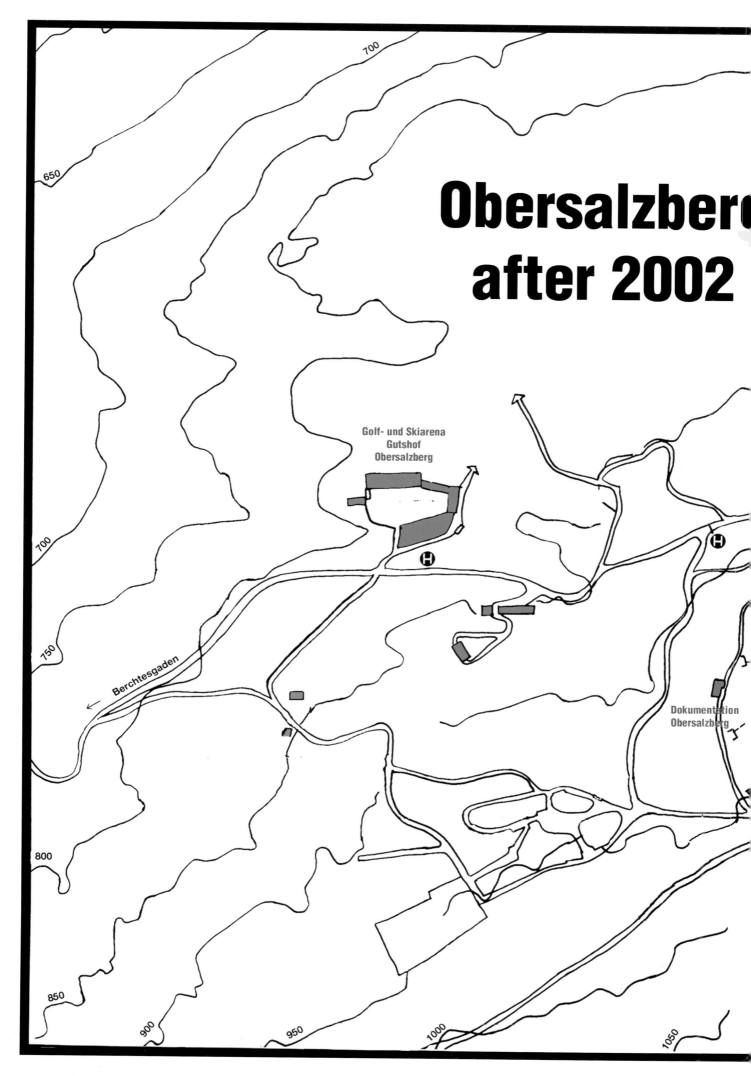

Obersalzber
after 2002

Golf- und Skiarena
Gutshof
Obersalzberg

Berchtesgaden

Dokumentation
Obersalzberg

650

700

700

750

800

850

900

950

1000

1050

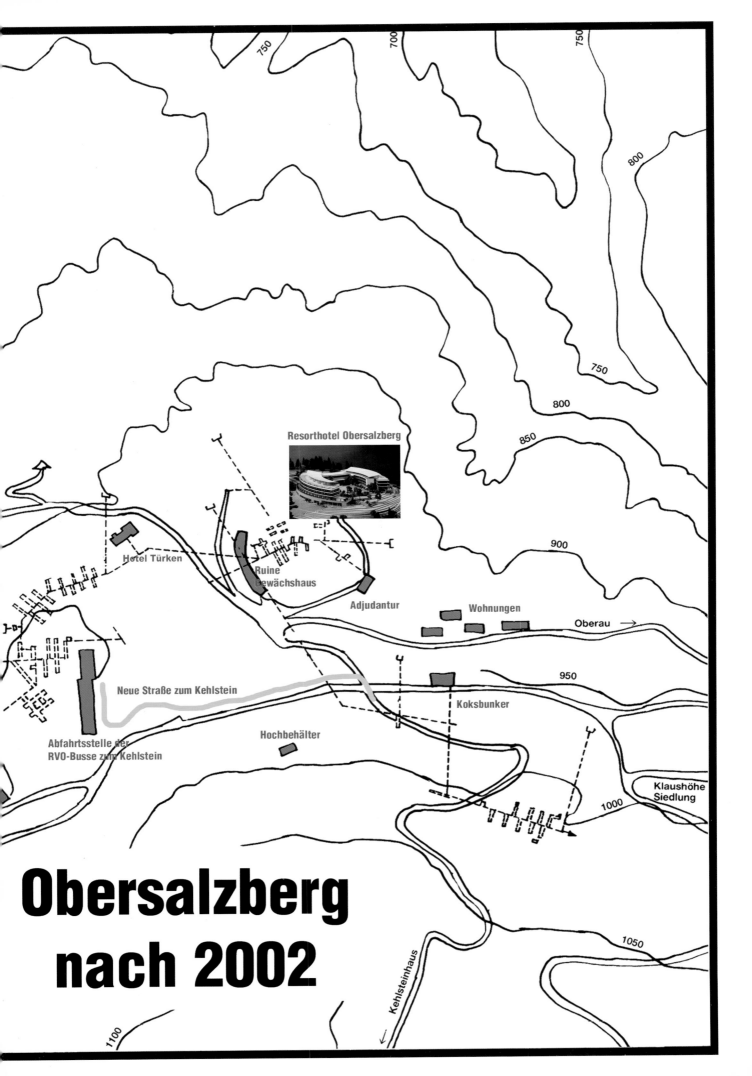

Resorthotel Obersalzberg

750

700

750

800

750

800

850

900

Hotel Türken

Ruine
Gewächshaus

Adjudantur

Wohnungen

Oberau →

950

Koksbunker

Neue Straße zum Kehlstein

Hochbehälter

Abfahrtsstelle der
RVO-Busse zum Kehlstein

Klaushöhe
Siedlung

1000

Obersalzberg
nach 2002

1050

1100

Kehlsteinhaus

Top: The hayrick of the Gutshof while used by Bormann. After the war, the Americans established a golf course and a skiing area here.

The original railway lines in the stable denote its former use. The lobby and a hall in the "Skytop Lodge" as they were left by the Americans:

The bombed-out house of Bormann (circle). In the foreground the ruins of the administration building, the barracks, the kindergarden and the model house for architectural planning.

Today the site of the house (circle) can really only be guessed. Strong spruce and bushes are growing on the grounds.

Bormannhouse   Türken hotel   Hitler`s Berghof

The Tuerken Hotel

The so-called „Tuerkenhaeusl" was situated in the imme-diate vicinity of the Berghof. According to accounts it was built by a veteran of the Turkish War on returning home. In 1903 the then warden of the Purtschellerhaus mountain hut on the Hoher Goell, Karl Schuster, bought the build-ing. He was a clever businessman and turned the house into a much-frequented restaurant with its own butcher´s shop. Just like the nearby Platterhof the restaurant "Zum Tuerken" became the meeting place of famous persons. Prince Regent Luitpold of Bavaria, Johannes Brahms, Clara Schumann, Peter Rosegger, Richard Voss and even Crown Princess Caecilie and Crown Prince Wilhelm of Prussia were among the visitors.

Due to disparaging remarks on the Nazi regime Karl Schus-ter got into trouble. He was forced to sell the house and sent to prison. When Bormann began to create the "Fuehrer´s restricted zone", the security service of the Reich (RSD) and the guards were quartered there. They used the build-ing until 1945.

In the bomb attack of April 25, 1945, the restaurant got badly damaged. Even though Karl Schuster´s daughter, Mrs Therese Partner, applied to the authorities for the re-turn of the house immediately after the collapse of the Third Reich, she could not prevent it from being looted. In 1946, under most difficult circumstances, she started to rebuild the house and save it from further dilapidation. In the front part of the house her efforts proved successful. But in 1947, on the order of the American authorities, the building had to be cleared for the second time. Again it was looted, and even built-in objects were removed.

It was only in March 1949 that, in connection with war reparation, Mrs Partner was finally granted ownership. The necessary settlement with the State of Bavaria was achieved on December 17, 1949. It gave the owner the chance to buy back the ruin as well as the underground bunker system "in the then condition". Disregarding all ob-jections, she began to furnish a flat and establish a café one year later.

Now as then the Tuerken Hotel is very popular on account of its site and its atmosphere. It is often mixed up with the Berghof because from its windows one gets the same view of Berchtesgaden and Salzburg as from Hitler´s house. The huge bunker system which is still in its original condition and part of which is open to the public is a special attrac-tion for many visitors.

Tuerken hotel

Tuerken

The greenhouse on t[

Top and right:
90% of the hotel´s structure
is original.

Hitler`s Berghof

Centre:
View from Bormann´s house of the
Tuerken Hotel and the Berghof.

Goering`s Hill"

Bottom:
The Tuerken Hotel /RDS (situated
above and very close to the Berghof) after the air-raid.

e`s Nest

SS Barracks

Garage Platterhof

Tuerken hotel

Hitler`s Berghof

The Theatre

In order to keep the thousands of workers happy Bormann had a theatre hall built. It was discussed a lot. Some thought it was a private cinema of Adolf Hitler, others suspected that there political propaganda was heaped upon the men working on the many building sites. It was, however, wrong to call the theatre Hitler´s personal movie palace. This cinema, with seats for 2000 people, could be visited by all the workers: Italians, Czechs, Poles and Ukrainians. Only few rows of seats were reserved for party bigwigs and their wives. The latest films featuring the then well-known actors were shown. Furthermore, there were cabaret shows and news-reels. Hitler entered the theatre only rarely.

It was constructed as a robust wooden building with a massive foundation which can still be seen. Outside, the house was covered with rough boards which went well with the landscape. Wooden benches served as seats. The technical equipment was modern. It is perhaps worth mentioning that the ceiling was lined with many lengths of heavy velvet, probably for reasons of acoustics.

Even though the house was constructed so as to take heavy snowfall the roof collapsed in a severe winter shortly after an evening performance. Nobody was injured.

The Guest-house

Reichsleiter Bormann had his office in the "Haus Hoher Goell". The guests here were mainly people who had something to do with him. After the "Anschluss" (Austria's incorporation into the Reich), VIP's were accommodated at the Palace of Klessheim between Salzburg and the German town of Freilassing. The ruins of the house were removed in 1995, leaving only the basement on which the new rooms of the "Dokumentation Obersalzberg, Orts- und Zeitgeschichte" were constructed. The exhibition was opened to the public on 20 Oct:, 1999, and has developed into a crowd-puller due to its excellent presentation of the ill-fated Nazi regime. through a glass connecting room you get to parts of the former bunker system.

The connecting building to the bunker system.

Top, right: The party guest-house before and after reconstruction.

The ruin was left to dilapidate.

Next page: "Dokumentation Obersalzberg, Orts- und Zeitgeschichte"; entrance to the exhibition.

Page 56: The theatre with the workers' huts to the south-east of Hintereck.

The Greenhouse

Bormann could never be stopped in his construction mania. Two examples are particularly odd.

He had a greenhouse erected specially in order to cater for the culinary well-being of the party bigwigs. The remains of the greenhouse, a curving wall below the new hotel, can still be seen.

Mountain soil and rough climate were totally unsuited for a market-garden, but this problem could be solved by money huge amounts of which Bormann obviously always had at his disposal. While the maxim "Plant vegetables instead of flowers!" reigned in the rest of Germany, the opposite was true for the Obersalzberg. A modern heating system provided the huge greenhouse with the proper climate. In

the basement of the two-storied building mushrooms were grown. When a heavy hailstorm broke the glass roof, it was assumed that it would not be repaired as long as the war lasted. Surely glass was needed more in the bombed-out cities than for covering plants. But this was not so. At that time Bormann stayed at the Fuehrer´s headquarters. One telegram was enough to get money from a fund intended for "special construction measures of the Fuehrer", and the necessary material was made available, too. The following account is another example of wastefulness. Hitler gave the order to protect nature during construction work. Deer were fed regularly, and hundreds of nesting boxes were erected.

Bormann wanted to show off again. He ordered to build an apiary for 100 bee colonies. When the site proved to be unsuited, he had another, much bigger apiary erected a little below the restricted zone. The building included a flat for the specially assigned warden and a room for his equipment.

Of course the population on the Obersalzberg steadily increased. In order to guarantee order and the safety of the bigwigs, a special security guard was established. It always accompanied Hitler. The security service of the Reich, RSD, was responsible for political matters. In an emergency, it was supplemented by a squad on guard. Bormann had the SS barracks built for the accommodation of these men. The barracks included an underground shooting range, a large barrack square, kitchen buildings, large cellars etc.

Goeringhill

Greenhouse

Barrack square

Goering´s Hill

Greenhouse

Guardhouse

Drivers´ garages

The Platterhof

There were crowds of visitors, on some days up to 5000, and they had to be fed and accommodated. Therefore Adolf Hitler gave the order to convert the Platterhof, formerly his favourite spot on the Obersalzberg, into a people´s hotel. Each "pilgrim" was to have the chance to stay near Hitler for one day and one night for only one Reichsmark. Construction work began in the summer of 1938. The Fuehrer really intended to build a simple hotel. Bormann, however, brought his influence to bear.

The formerly modest house of Mauritia Mayer, the founder of tourism in the Berchtesgadener Land, was once again changed. During construction work Bormann behaved abominably. Again and again he uttered new wishes which resulted in big changes. People were afraid of him and nobody dared to tell him about the limits of technical possibilities. At the beginning of the war it was declared a "building programme of the Fuehrer which was important for the war". So were most of Bormann´s other buildings. Thus Hitler became commander-in-chief and Bormann got absolute control over construction work on the Obersalzberg. He drove everybody to best performance. Once, mad with rage, he threw the model of the building - it had cost 20 000 Reichsmark - to the floor so that it was destroyed. In the end the hotel contained every

conceivable luxury. Heavy carpets and precious paintings, a mirror hall, a library, a large coffee hall the ceiling of which had cost more than 20.000 Reichsmark, a bombproof skittle-alley, guest rooms with a total of 159 beds.

Gilding the sign "Hotel Platterhof" kept artisans busy for several months. Eventually, Bormann did not like it and it was stored away.

After completion the building was not a people´s hotel but, according to the then standards, a luxury hotel, and no common man could have afforded to stay there.
During the air-raid the Platterhof was badly damaged (see next two pages). Today nothing is left of the Platterhof, later "General Walker Hotel". Apart from the "Skyline Room" (formerly terrace hall), it has been completely removed. The remains of its walls were filled into caves of the underground bunker system beneath the barracks grounds. On that spot, a large car park has been built as the buses to the Eagle´a Nest depart from here.

60

Moritz Mayer Hof (Judit Platter)
Berchtesgaden Obersalzberg

The badly damaged Platterhof
after the air-raid of 1945.

The central area of the Obersalzberg with its former buildings - an expanse of rubble. The picture was taken by American tourists in about 1953. The shooting range beneath the barracks was not damaged.

Bottom, left:
The house where the employees of the Platterhof lived. It was later demolished, only the first floor was left and used as a garage. The ruins of the Platterhof were demolished, only the back wall was left standing. It served as a supporting wall to the slope where the buses to the Eagle´s Nest depart.

The remains of the Platterhof in 2000. Today this is a car park.

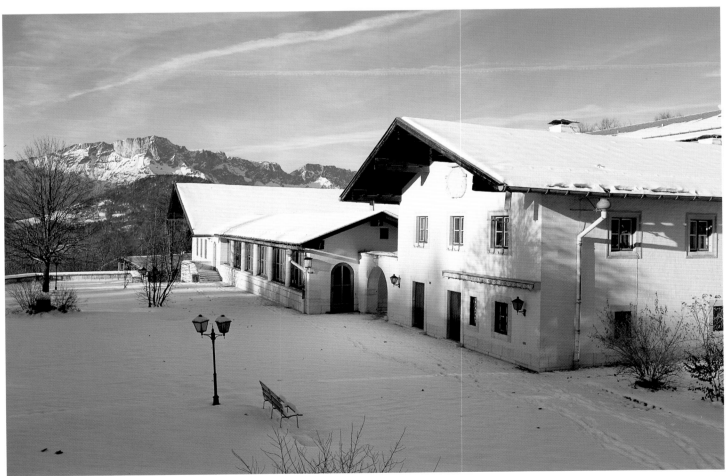

Page 66:
The Platterhof was rebuilt in its original form after the war. The hotel served members of the US forces and their families as a holiday resort and gained world-wide renown. It was demolished in 2000. For the Berchtesgaden business world the visitors had constituted an important economic factor.

Top:
The former barracks in 2001. The basement has been uncovered, holes are being filled and everything is being renaturalized.

Remains of the greenhouse. In the foreground the new route of the road up to the Eagle's Nest (Kehlsteinstrasse).

The Eagle´s Nest

The Kehlsteinhaus, or D-House, on the top of the Kehlstein (1843m) is doubtlessly one of the most interesting buildings constructed under Bormann. Erroneously often called "Teahouse", it was given the name Eagle´s Nest by the Americans. It probably was also that imaginary Alpine fort that the Allies wanted to take in 1945.

The Hoher Goell rises steeply directly behind the house, which gives the scenery an extremely alpine character. The road leads from Hintereck up to a height of 1700 metres, with only a single bend. Every meter of the road had to be wrenched from the hard rock - a strenuous task. Many workers lost their lives. Bormann, as usual, urged everybody to hurry up.

The road ends in a big car park from which a 3-metre-high and 124-metre-long tunnel leads to an elevator. Bormann´s lavish furnishings can be seen here, too. Door handles made of massive brass, an elevator lined with brass, and heavy copper doors were used in this tunnel lined with natural stones.

The elevator covers another 124 meters and ends in the interior of the house. The Eagle´s Nest is not particularly large. It consists of a study, dining-room, living-room, kitchen, room for relaxation, bathrooms and a large basement. The rooms are panelled with pine or elm wood. In the tea room Untersberg as well as Carrara marble were used.

The house was connected to the electricity system of Berchtesgaden, but it also had a special generator from a German submarine for emergencies. The heating system was in the tunnel leading to the elevator.
Why was so much trouble taken? Did Bormann want to make a special present to Hitler, or was it rather a means of self-affirmation for the "genius" Bormann?

Officially it was to serve as accommodation for high-ranking guests. Hitler visited the Eagle´s Nest only five times, Bormann used it much more often. It is also to be mentioned that it was never used for military purposes and was not constructed to that end, either. Governor Jacob prevented it from being blown up. The house was spared. It was handed over to the German Alpine Club which still rents it to be used as a mountain restaurant.

Special RVO buses run to the car park below the Eagle´s Nest several times a day. From the car park the original elevator can be used. This trip is recommendable because of the exceptionally beautiful panorama. The view goes from Salzburg over the Berchtesgadener Land to Lake Koenigssee and the Steinernes Meer. From Hintereck, the road is closed to private cars.

Picture in an American leaflet on the situation of the Eagle´s Nest.

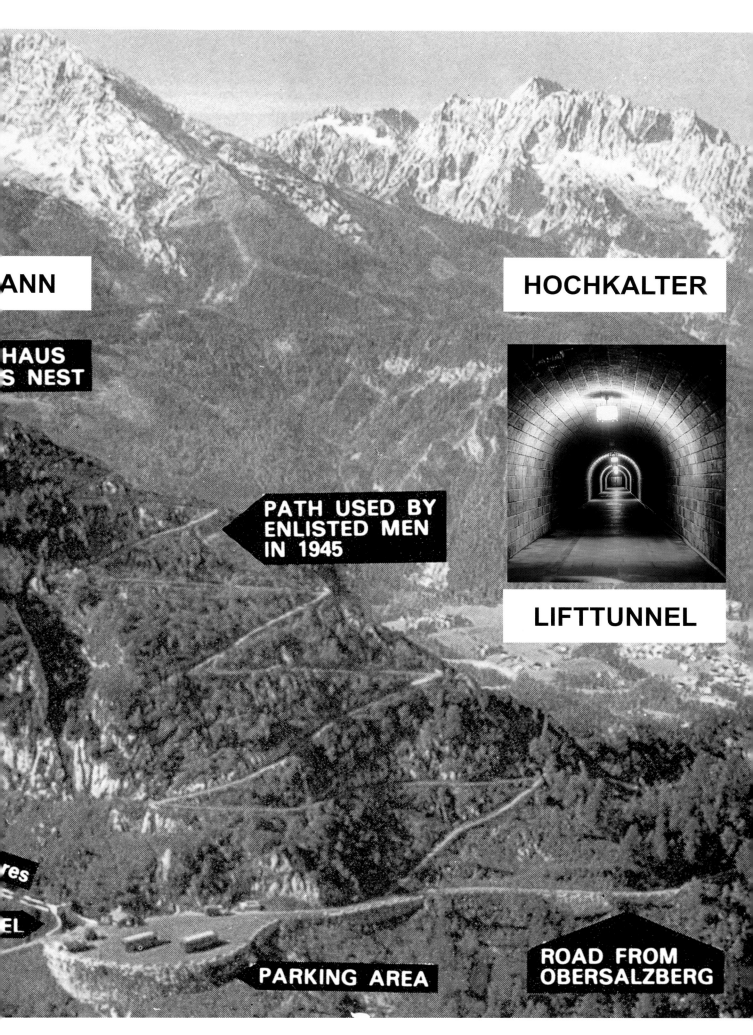

ANN

HAUS
S NEST

HOCHKALTER

PATH USED BY
ENLISTED MEN
IN 1945

LIFTTUNNEL

res

EL

PARKING AREA

ROAD FROM
OBERSALZBERG

Several tunnels had to be blasted
into the rock. Construction work
was done in a hurry.
Accidents were inevitable.

Top, right:
Building material was transported
to the building site of the Eagle´s Nest
by cable-cars. The building is really
massive but not very large.
Due to its situation in the high
mountains the house is only
accessible, or free of snow,
in the summer months.

Page 71:
The Eagle´s Nest is lined with
granite and looks just like
the surrounding rocks.

The Eagle´s Nest in 1995.

The Eagle´s Nest, a building site
in the high mountains. The wooden
scaffolding jutted out
over sheer drops.

The fantastic situation of the Eagle´s Nest, with a panoramic view from Lake Königssee to the Watzmann, the Hochkalter, the Untersberg to the city of Salzburg and the Rossfeld mountain.

The single bend of the Kehlstein Road.
The Watzmann in the background.

A present of Mussolini to Hitler: the open chimney
in the tearoom, made of Carrara marble.

Untersberg

Klaushoehe

At that time, building material was stored at the large car park below the road leading to the tollgate on the southern side of the Rossfeld Road. The car park was intended for all kinds of vehicles. During the former motorcar races on the Rossfeld it served as a drivers´ camp.

The Obersalzberg centre is about 1 km away from here. After about 500 meters, the road passes the former coke bunker. 30 000 hundredweights of coke were stored there. After invasion, the Allies set fire to the coke which continued to glimmer until October.

The Nazi regime wanted the Klaushoehe to be appreciated as a great feat of social commitment. There were four rows of 8 houses each, with each house containing 2 or 3 comfortable apartments. They were furnished with modern kitchens and bathrooms and were equivalent to apartments of higher officials in towns. This was really the first attempt to settle the Obersalzberg with people loyal to the party line. The apartments were not allocated to those who needed them most, but only to those who were on good terms with Hitler or Bormann. Rent was accordingly low.

The bomb attack destroyed many of the buildings, and there was looting as well. Partly they had to be demolished. Houses that were still inhabitable were allocated to displaced persons after World War II.

Buchenhoehe

This was the second largest settlement on the Obersalzberg. Only members of site supervision knew that something special was to be built here, as the plan was officially declared secret. Construction work was extremely difficult. The rock was covered with detritus mixed with loam and interspersed with big boulders, or sometimes with so-called "Haselgebirge". Both kinds of ground have the same characteristics: when dry they can only be worked with pneumatic hammers, when wet they become mud. Particularly deep and strong foundations had to be erected, reinforced by much more iron than usual. In winter workers arrived in truck-loads to remove the snow. Buildings which were already under construction were covered with tents and heated by steam. Hundreds of thousands of m³ of earth had to be moved. Streams were diverted to run 30 - 40 meters lower down, and parts of the forests were cleared.

About 40 houses containing 2 - 4 apartments, with each apartment consisting of 5 - 8 rooms, were built. Moreover, a department store with cold store rooms, a restaurant, a kindergarten with terraced hall, an outdoor swimming pool, a school, a gym, large garages, a transformer station, a building for the fire brigade and a big heating system were erected. The heating system was to supply all apartments with warm water and hot air.

Constructing all these buildings required exceptionally huge amounts of money and material. People were amazed. But the war left its signs here, too. For the first time Bormann had great difficulties in obtaining material. Minister of the Reich Albert Speer kept asking Bormann to stop construction work. But Bormann knew how to continue by referring to Hitler´s orders. The bomb attack of April 25 set an end to it.

The Underground Bunker System

In 1943 aerial warfare in Germany was intensified. Towns were bombed and thousands of people died in the ruins. Many lost their homes, and misery descended upon Germany. For reasons of propaganda the term "antiaircraft defence" was not well liked on the Obersalzberg. Bormann did not take any steps in this direction, either. But all of a sudden, in August 1943, the terms "tunnel" and "safety of the Fuehrer" were pronounced by everybody. Hurriedly plans for a huge bunker system on the Obersalzberg were drafted. Apart from essential items it was to contain a lot of luxury.

Meanwhile Minister of the Reich Albert Speer managed to draft some of the younger workers. They were replaced by Czechs and Italians. In the end only 30 % of the workers were Germans. The fact that many different languages were spoken made work difficult. The following description of the bunker system is taken from the book "Obersalzberg" by Josef Geiß:

"A straight tunnel or a flight of steps led so far away from the entrance that there was a sufficient covering of about 30 to 50 meters. Then there was a buffer-stop to absorb the impact at bomb explosions. Behind it there were gas locks from which the tunnels led on into the interior of the mountain (see picture p. 76). Caverns were on both sides of the tunnels.

Under most of the tunnels there were galleries containing pipes for ventilation, water, electricity, sewage and warm air for heating. The buffer-stops contained chambers for fixing machine guns. The rock was partly solid, but especially Hitler´s tunnel system showed crumbling rock interspersed with loam, so that every tunnel had to be reinforced with

wooden beams. Later the tunnels were concreted. The lining of the excavated tunnels was very carefully planned. A concrete shell of about 30 - 60 cm was fixed to the rock wall. Then followed a layer of cement and an insulating layer consisting of a kind of roofing felt or artificial rubber. Next to this insulating layer was a 25-cm-thick wall. Ground water could seep through the concrete shell (by means of built-in special stones) and conducted to the sewers through which it ran off. There were strong iron doors at the entrances. Goering was the only man on the Obersalzberg who had had his own bunker system constructed under his house earlier. The first systems were intended for Hitler, Eva Braun, adjutants and guests. Another system was made available to Bormann and his family. The Berghof system was the first on which work was started. It was to be completed by Christmas Eve 1943, when Hitler would visit the Obersalzberg. Due to the crumbling rock the beginning of work was delayed so that in the end the air-raid shelter had to be completed in only eight weeks."

Another excerpt from the book of Josef Geiß, who during the war held a job with the administration of construction work and thus gained an extensive insight into the events on the Obersalzberg:

"Work was started on the bunker system of the Berghof. A certain section was to be completed by December 24, 1943, as Hitler was expected then. The beginning of construction work was delayed. The reason for this was the crumbly condition of the ground. All available aid was used. The date was kept by extraordinary hurrying. Masons, standing side by side in the tunnel, were working on the arches. Between their legs the labourers were crawling on all fours, bringing mortar and sto-nes.Carpenters, the workers responsible for the insulating layer, electricians, the men working on the telephone line and plumbers also had to find some room inside the tunnel. It was terribly cramped. Thus the 130-meter-long tunnel including caves was completed in only eight week "Work was started on the bunker system of the Berghof. A certain section was to be completed by December 24, 1943, as Hitler was expected then. The beginning of construction work was delayed. The reason for this was the crumbly con-

Picture p. 76:
Way down to the bunkers with opening for machine guns at the end of the steps. The two levels of a half-completed tunnel. Below the floor were the supply tunnels. There are caverns on both sides.

The large machine room
in the bunker.

dition of the ground. All available aid was used. The date was kept by extraordinary hurrying. Masons, standing side by side in the tunnel, were working on the arches. Between their legs the labourers were crawling on all fours, bringing mortar and stones.Carpenters, the workers responsible for the insulating layer, electricians, the men working on the telephone line and plumbers also had to find some room inside the tunnel. It was terribly cramped. Thus the 130-meter-long tunnel including caves was completed in only eight week from the first mix of concrete to the polished parquet floor, panelling and furnishing.

Originally it was planned to build simple air-raid shelters. But then special wishes were uttered. The security service demanded the installation of machine guns. For artistic reasons the architects did not want to do without marble, precious wood panelling, air conditioning, carpets, dressing rooms etc. Bormann wanted to have the headquarters situated lower down; Goering demanded that his own air-raid shelter be connected with the bunker system. But when this actually was to be carried out, Bormann refused to have his section connected with the tunnel of the Reichsmarschall. Thus the two systems did not meet 10 meters of ground remained between them. Now the ventilation machines were insufficient. Further excavations had to be made. When everything was finished, somebody remembered that one chamber had been forgotten. Excavations started anew. Then various janitors came. They needed store rooms. The dog keeper needed an extra room for Hitler´ German shepherd dog. Then there were great misgivings as to whether dog hair held gas and whether a special ventilation system was to be installed instead of using simple filters. The people responsible for the installation of the telephone found that the cables were not big enough which led to further excavations.

Eva Braun was not prepared to do without a bath tub. The cooks demanded fully furnished kitchens. Special chambers for paintings and records and libraries had to be made. Bormann got his own air-raid dining-room. In the end, shortly before the completion of the air-raid shelter, anti-aircraft headquarters wanted their own bunker. Then an emergency power generator had to be installed, too, which actually did not work during the bomb attack.

Top: The entrance doors consisted of heavy iron. This entrance lies opposite the guard house near the Tuerken Hotel. To the left of the door, people keen on getting into the bunker have made a hole.

Bottom: The entrance of a tunnel from the inside. Seeping ground water has created long stalactites.

In addition there were the bunkers at Buchenhoehe and the large air-raid shelter of the Gutshof, but neither was completely finished. Bormann was not content with the air-raid shelters allotted to him since Goering was not modest, either. He claimed a number of chambers of the anti-aircraft headquarters for himself. There he put up rows of closets filled with silver chandeliers, silver tableware, jewellery, huge amounts of clothes, among them his famous 36 tailored suits and uniforms. Food was stored, too: fat, sugar, flour, canned food. Bormann stored so much in his bunker that according to estimates he and his family could have lived and clothed themselves for 200 years.

The bunkers were lavishly furnished: The parquet floors were covered with heavy carpets. The walls boasted expensive panelling. Doors and door frames were brightly varnished. In the kitchens there were combined stoves, and the washing rooms and bathrooms were also luxuriously furnished. A telephone system with 800 connections was just sufficient. The offices were furnished with hard-wood furniture, heavy desks, roll-fronted cupboards, leather chairs etc. Steel cupboards, built into the rock, were also there. The living-rooms, bedrooms and children's rooms resembled those above ground. The workers and the "ordinary" people on the Obersalzberg had to do with 385 m². More than 1000 people were packed in half-completed shelters.

The safe in Bormann´s air-raid shelter. It was too heavy to be removed by looters.

Page 81, top:
View of the aerial foundations of the former flight control center inside the Obersalzberg. In the background the barracks in 2002.

Page 81, bottom:
Site of the emergency generator. Today some of the tunnels can be visited in connection with the exhibition "Dokumentation Obersalzberg".

81

Occupation

A man with a vision and a good heart was able to prevent the worst for Berchtesgaden at that time. Governor Theodor Jacob early realized the danger which Hitler and his party friends on the Obersalzberg presented. When things got increasingly threatening for Berchtesgaden, he pressed for a decision. Under all conditions did Jacob want to surrender Berchtesgaden without a fight.

During the morning the news came from Bad Reichenhall that this town had been surrendered to the Americans. By tele-phone, the Governor had the commander-in-chief notified that the community of Bischofswiesen and the market town of Berchtesgaden would show no resistance. A hurriedly published leaflet reassured the population and appealed to the people to keep calm. The former Governor, holding a white flag of capitulation in his hand, went to meet the American troops. At the level-crossing gates at Winkl the Berchtesgadener Land was handed over to the commander of the tank group. At the head of the unit Governor Jacob went back to Berchtesgaden - probably the hardest trip of his life. They stopped at the Castle Square and after some discussion went on to have a look at the Obersalzberg. The SS commander on the Obersalzberg had long been against Hitler and did not fall back on his word given to the Governor. He dissolved the SS and dismissed his soldiers. The Volks-sturm was also dissolved.

In the afternoon tanks of the 101 Airborn Division rolled through Bischofswiesen and Berchtesgaden. The population had hoisted white flags. American tanks also came from the direction of Salzburg. The French hurried across Pass Hirschbichl and were the first on the Obersalzberg. The coal bunker was set on fire; it was to glow until the middle of October. Blind rage of destruction began to spread. In the following days the same thing was to be seen everywhere. Soldiers were billeted, for which reason houses were cleared. The military government was housed in Wittelsbacher Castle. The French troops with their Moroccan units made themselves especially unpopular. They were accused of the worst offences against civilians.

American soldiers in the ruins of the Berghof.

Platterhof

Barrack square

Bormann`s house

Hitler`s Berghof

The remains of the Obersalzberg; today it is not possible to take a comparable picture from the same position.

The ground is overgrown with big beech hedges, bushes and spruce.

Hotel Tuerken

Hitler´s Berghof

The Obersalzberg today

The Obersalzberg with the Eagle´s Nest is one of the most popular destinations for excursions in the Berchtesgadener Land. The view from the top of the Kehlstein (1843m) is unique.

From 1953 onwards, the former Platterhof was used as "General Walker Hotel", an "Armed Forces Recreation Center". Among the members of the US forces it obtained world-wide renown. In 1996, in connection with a reduction of troops, the US forces withdrew from the Obersalzberg. In 1999 demolition work began.

On the Eckerbichl, formerly "Goering´s Hill", a luxury hotel was built (see colour picture). The underground rifle-ranges and bunkers were uncovered and the rubble left after the demolition of the Platterhof was filled into holes. The whole area has been renaturalized.

Millionen im Fels

Wiedererschließung des Obersalzbergs · Die Hochalpenstraße Berchtesgadens und die Möglichkeiten ihrer Ausnützung

In Berchtesgaden wurde in letzter Zeit einiges erreicht, das nicht nur für die kommende Saison, sondern für den Fremdenverkehr überhaupt von Bedeutung ist. Die Lähmung der Kriegs- und Nachkriegsjahre ist — ähnlich wie während der Einführung der Rentenmark in den Jahren 1924 bis 1929 — durch die wachsende Aktivität einer neuen wirtschaftlichen Entwicklung überwunden.

Es war allerhöchste Zeit, einen Ansatzpunkt zum Besseren zu schaffen. Berchtesgaden lief Gefahr, alte, treue Kurgäste zu verlieren, und solche, die zum erstenmal kamen, von einer Wiederholung des Besuches abzuschrecken. Es waren nicht Hunderte, sondern Tausende, die während der letzten Jahre empört fragten: „Wozu müssen wir ihr eigentlich Kurtaxe zahlen?" Sie hatten nicht unrecht: Kein Kurpark, keine Kurkapelle, nicht einmal Bänke an den Spazierwegen (sie waren längst verfeuert und wurden dank der Bemühungen der Kurdirektion nach der Währungsreform allmählich wieder aufgestellt) und die wenigen Omnibuslinien zu den Ausflugszielen der Umgebung so überfüllt, daß kaum die einheimischen Berufstätigen mitkommen konnten. Es blieben nur der Königsee und das Salzbergwerk als traditionelle Anziehungspunkte des Berchtesgadener Fremdenverkehrs ohne merkliche Einschränkungen der von früher her gewohnten Verkehrsverhältnisse.

Seitdem hat sich über den allgemeinen Wandel hinaus einiges zugunsten des Berchtesgadener und ihrer Gäste geändert. Es ist die allmähliche Wiedererschließung des Obersalzbergs und seiner weiteren Umgebung für den öffentlichen Verkehr. Die Hänge, die von der Linie Roßfeld - Oberau - Unterau bis hinüber nach Vorderbrand und zum Jenner das Berchtesgadener Tal östlich und südlich begrenzen, haben für den Fremdenverkehr eine stets wachsende Bedeutung gewonnen, seit in den siebziger Jahren des vorigen

es im Gegensatz zu anderen Zielen keines langen Anmarsches bedurfte, da ja die Hänge des Obersalzbergs unmittelbar aus dem Ort Berchtesgaden aufsteigen. Mit dem Ausbau der Vorderecker Straße wurde die Entwicklung weiter gefördert. Das alljährliche Autorennen, wäre während dem Namen Obersalzberg über Deutschland hinaus bekannt. Schließlich konnte man mit Raupenschleppern bis zum Eckersattel und zum Roßfeld fahren.

Dann kamen die Jahre des „Dritten Reiches", der Zwangsaufkäufe, der Schließung der Fremdenbetriebe, der Vernichtung jahrhundertealter Bauernhöfe und immer weiter um sich greifenden Ausdehnung des hermetisch abgeschlossenen „Führersperrgebietes".

Die Erbschaft waren Trümmer, Bombenkrater und - etwas sehr Wertvolles: ein weit verzweigtes Netz moderner Hochgebirgsstraßen, wie sie sich Berchtesgaden aus eigener Kraft unter normalen Verhältnissen nie hätte leisten können. Diesen einzigen positiven Teil einer belastenden Erbschaft verkommen zu lassen, wäre sündhafter Frevel. Es ist hier im Großen, wie bei einem Blechdach im Kleinen. Läßt man es rosten, statt den Schutzfarbe zu erneuern, dann wird aus einer verschobenen Reparatur um einige Hundert Mark in etlichen Jahren eine zwingend notwendige, die einige Tausend verschlingt.

Leider wurde hier schon manches versäumt, und es ist viel nachzuholen. Millionenwerte stehen auf dem Spiel. Nur ein Beispiel: Auf der Strecke Endstal - Ligeret - Kehlsteinstraße sind schon ernstliche Schäden festzustellen, und herabgestürzte Blöcke versperren seit längerer Zeit stellenweise den

So weit war in den letzten Tagen vor Kriegsausbruch die Hochalpenstraße in der Nähe des Ahornkaser in 1700 Meter Höhe bereits gediehen.

Jahrhunderts Moritz Mayer in mutiger Pionierarbeit gegen viele feindliche Widerstände als ersten Fremdenbetrieb aus dem ehemaligen Steinhauslehen die Pension Moritz machte. Richard Voß verewigte in seinem berühmten Roman „Zwei Menschen" diese Pension Moritz unter dem Namen Platterhof. Andere folgten dem Beispiel der beiwilligen, schöpferischen Frau, und aus einer abgelegenen Bergbauerngemeinde wurde der Obersalzberg allmählich zu einem beliebten, vielbesuchten Fremdenziel. Es entstand ein Netz von gepflegten Spazierwegen. Hochlenzer — Scharitzkehl — Vorderbrand über den oberen und unteren Lindeweg nach der einen, die Wasserleitungswege und der Weg über die zwei Stollen zur Au nach der anderen Seite gehörten bald zu den landschaftlich schönsten Ausflügen der näheren Umgebung. Das touristische Hinterland des Göllstockes mit seinen Ausläufern bot von der leichten Almwanderung zu den Ahornkasern mit weitem Blick nach Oesterreich hinein bis zur äußerst schwierigen Klettertour in der Westwand des Hohen Göll lohnende Ziele für jeden Geschmack.

Der starke Besuch dieses Gebietes war nicht zuletzt der Tatsache zu verdanken, daß

Die Kehlsteinstraße nach dem ersten Tunnel mit Blick auf Watzmann, Hundstod und Steinernes Meer.

(Aufnahmen 2 - 6 H. Schöner)

Weg. Wenn sich niemand findet, sie wegzuräumen, so ist das die Dauer ein beschämender Zustand für den Kurort Berchtesgaden.

Diese Straßen liegen auch nach Beseitigung des „Führersperrgebietes" aus zwei Gründen für den deutschen Zivilverkehr brach und tun es zum Teil noch:

1. Der Mangel an Fahrzeugen und Treibstoff behinderte die nach den Bedürfnissen entsprechende Ausdehnung des Omnibusverkehrs. Erst in diesem Jahr wurden durch die neuen, bzw. verbesserten und noch verbesserungsbedürftigen Kraftpostlinien zum Pechhäusl und zur Klaushöhe ein erster Schritt vorwärts getan und wenigstens der äußerste linke Flügel des Obersalzberg-Straßennetzes endlich wieder dem öffentlichen Verkehr zugänglich gemacht.

In der irrigen Beförderung, die Deutschen hätten nach dem Zusammenbruch keine anderen Sorgen, als zu den Trümmern des Obersalzbergs trauernd wallfahren zu gehen, hielten die Amerikaner einen Teil des ehemaligen „Führersperrgebietes" bis heute verschlossen, ein Rezept, das sich nicht immer bewährt. Durch ein geheimnisvolles Sperrgebiet wird eher das Gegenteil dessen er-

reicht, was bezweckt ist. Die zuständigen amerikanischen Stellen scheinen das erkannt zu haben, denn neulich sprach Landwirtschaftsminister Dr. Schlögl in Berchtesgaden davon, daß er bald das „Erbe des Obersalzbergs" zu übernehmen habe.

Das Sperrgebiet des Obersalzbergs ist bereits verkleinert und erfreulich gelockert. Durch die EBAG-Linie nach Scharitzkehl — Göllhäusl wurde es erstmals für den öffentlichen Verkehr durchbrochen. Durch das Seilbahnprojekt, dessen Verwirklichung immer näher rückt, gewinnt die kurz unterhalb des Jennerfeldes laufende Querstraße an Bedeutung. Ein weiterer erfreulicher Schritt zur Wiedererschließung des Obersalzberges wird es sein, wenn in Kürze der unrentable Gutshof-Fremdenbetrieb und Gaststätte wird.

Das Wichtigste ist aber, mit dem Salzberg auch den Kehlstein freizubekommen. Hierfür sprechen so eindeutig wirtschaftliche Argumente, daß sich ihnen in einer Zeit krisenhafter Wirtschaftslage auch die Amerikaner nicht dauernd verschließen können. Die Kehlsteinstraße ist die großartigste Hochalpenstraße auf deutschem Boden. Sie ist nicht mit der Gaisbergstraße Salzburgs, sondern bestenfalls mit der Großglocknerstraße zu vergleichen und allein dadurch eine Fremdenverkehrsattraktion ersten Ranges. Der Durchbruch durch die Südwestabstürze des Kehlsteins mit den Tunnels und Kehren in der steilen Wand und dem grandiosen Einblick in die wild zerklüftete, 1200 Meter hohe Westflanke des Hohen Gölls ist eine technische Glanzleistung neuzeitlichen Straßenbaues, den berühmten Bergstraßen Österreichs, der Schweiz und Italiens ebenbürtig

Der alte Obersalzberg mit Kindersanatorium zur Seitz (Mitte), hintereck (rechts), Ebnerlehen (links) und dem Bohnerlehen und Bohnerfeld im Vordergrund. Mit Ausnahme der von Bormann übernommenen Villa Seitz links oben am Waldrand wurden die Häuser nach dem Zwangsaufkauf alle abgerissen. An dieser Stelle einstiger Schönheit erstreckt sich heute das Trümmerfeld der SS-Kasernen. (Aufn. L. Ammon)

Blick auf den Kehlstein mit dem sogenannten „Teehaus" und den Hohen Göll.

ist. Kein Kurgast des Berchtesgadener Landes würde sich einen Besuch des Kehlsteins entgehen lassen. Er wäre ein ebenso selbstverständlicher Programmpunkt wie der Königssee und das Salzbergwerk.

Der entscheidende Faktor liegt in der wirtschaftlichen Auswirkung dieser Anziehungskraft. Es ist nämlich bei solchen Bergstraßen, die unter einem außergewöhnlichen Aufwand als Mittel gebaut wurden, üblich, von allen Benützern, die in Omnibussen oder Privatfahrzeugen die Strecke benützen, eine Mautgebühr zu verlangen. Dadurch könnten die Mittel zur Unterhaltung des Obersalzberg-Straßennetzes und allmählich zusätzlich Gelder zur Fertigstellung der Roßfeld- und Dürreckstraße beschafft werden. Jede Verzögerung um eine Saison bedeutet einen unersetzlichen Verlust für ganz Berchtesgaden, dessen Existenzgrundlage, den Fremdenverkehr. Es steht außer jedem Zweifel, daß sich auf einer öffentlichen Benützung freigegebenen Kehlsteinstraße nicht nur eine häufig befahrene Kraftpostlinie rentieren würde, sondern daß darüber hinaus zahlreiche Ausflugsomnibusse und Kraftfahrzeuge von auswärts speziell wegen dieser in Deutschland einzigartigen Bergstraße nach Berchtesgaden kommen würden.

Im unbeschädigten „Adlerhorst" mit seiner herrlichen Terrasse gegen Göll, Königssee, Steinernes Meer und Watzmann kann ohne besondere Unkosten ein Berghotel untergebracht werden, das sich durch erstklassige Bewirtschaftung einen guten Ruf verschafft und dessen Ueberschuß ebenfalls der Unterhaltung des Straßennetzes und der Fertigstellung der anderen, durch den Krieg unterbrochenen Straßenbauten dienen kann.

Im Gegensatz zum Seilbahnprojekt, das nun endlich von einer eigens hierzu geschaffenen Körperschaft vertreten wird, gibt es bei einer Lösung der Frage: „Was wird aus dem Kehlstein?" keine Finanzierungsprobleme. Die Straßen sind da. Das künftige Berghotel steht ebenfalls oben in 1800 Meter Höhe. Es handelt sich hier nicht darum, Neues zu schaffen, sondern bereits Bestehendes seiner zweckentsprechenden Verwendung zuzuführen.

Es sei damit nicht gesagt, daß es nicht wünschenswert ist, auch einiges Neue zu schaffen. Eine Freigabe des Kehlsteins soll auch Touristen, Skifahrern und Bergsteigern zugute kommen. Im Vergleich zu dem, was bereits gebaut ist, bedarf es nur verhältnismäßig geringen Aufwandes, durch einen gut versicherten, vom Frühjahr bis in den Spätherbst begehbaren Steig über die Mandlköpfe und den waagerechten Abfall des Hohen Gölls oberhalb den Steilabbrüchen der Westwand den Anschluß an den Hauptweg herzustellen, dessen Ausläufer der Kehlstein ist. Der ermüdende Anstieg zum Göll als einer der beliebtesten hochalpinen Frühjahrsskitouren würde dadurch zu einer bequemen Wanderung. Während des Sommers wäre der Kehlstein Ausgangspunkt für Göll- und Brettüberschreitungen, und für Westwandkletterer eine günstig gelegene Abstiegs- und Rückfahrgelegenheit. Die Errichtung einer solchen Steiganlage durch eine gemeinsame Anstrengung der alpinen, Sport- und Fremdenver-

... und 1949: Kostspielige Bauten, die schon weitgehend fertiggestellt waren, liegen nun seit Jahren dem Verfall preisgegeben. Ein Torso der geplanten Hochalpenstraße im Schliefsteinboden bei Vorderbrand. Im Hintergrund der Kehlstein.

kehrsverbände würde die Unkosten durch erhöhte Einnahmen in Form von Mautgebühren wieder hereinbringen.

Millionen schlummern im Fels. Sie stammen aus deutscher Arbeitskraft, bezahlt mit deutschem Volksvermögen. Sie tragen keine Zinsen. Ihr Kapitalwert verringert sich durch unnützes Brachliegen.

Die Amerikaner sind im „Business" aufgewachsen. Mehr als andere Besatzungsmächte haben sie Verständnis für wirtschaftliche Notwendigkeiten. Mit der nötigen Ausdauer läßt sich sicher manches erreichen. Obersalzberg und Kehlstein wurden zwar 1945 dem Viermächte-Kontrollrat unterstellt; das entscheidende Machtwort haben hier in ihrer Zone aber doch die Amerikaner.

Es ist daher nicht nur Aufgabe, sondern Pflicht aller Behörden, Organisationen und Einzelpersonen, die Berchtesgadener Interessen zu vertreten haben, unermüdlich immer wieder vorstellig zu werden, die Obersalzberg und Kehlstein nach mehr als zehnjähriger Existenz für Privilegierte Gemeingut des Volkes. Sch.

Die Dürreckstraße gegen Hundstod, Watzmann und Hocheisspitze. Diese Teilstrecke der Hochalpenstraße ist eine der schönsten, weil sie einen grandiosen Blick in das von den 1200 m hohen Göll-Westwand überragte Endstal vermittelt.